written by
Joseph Johns[on]

Sid th[e]

The S[eal that]

Surfed

To my children Harmony & Avi.
Dream big and stay true to you.
- J.J

To Beth and Jonah for always
being there for me and
supporting me, I love you both.
And I guess to our cats,
who didn't do anything useful,
but still should get a mention.

-J.F

It was a warm
and sunny day
in the beautiful town
of Newquay,
the perfect weather
for surfing.

As the surfers paddled out to the break, they noticed a curious creature bobbing amongst the waves...

Sid was a regular in the waters of Newquay and was quite the local celebrity.

However, Sid was a bit of an oddity amongst the other seals, being a seal who loved to surf.

Sid didn't fit in with the other seals.

They would leave him out and joke amongst themselves about "Sid the Silly seal that thinks he can surf"!

Sid was often sad and alone but he did have his two best friends who believed in him; Gary the Gull and Jean Claude the Clam.

Everynight Sid would
be found counting
down the hours
until dawn break,
so once again he could
join the line up
and surf the
magnificent waves!

Sid had quickly become a mascot for the surfers who were always delighted to see him bobbing amongst the waves...

Sid was a natural
on the waves,
effortlessly gliding along
with his sleek body
and powerful flippers.

His fellow surfers often commented on how graceful he looked in the water.

Sid had a friendly and playful nature.

He loved to show off his surfing skills to the humans, riding the whitewash right up to the shoreline where the spectators gathered!

Gary the Gull
and Jean Claude the Clam
could often be found

gazing in amazement
as Sid would rip on
the waves!

Many people wondered how Sid had become such a talented surfer. Some speculated that he had been abandoned as a pup and raised by surfers,

As the years passed, Sid became a beloved part of the town and was fully embraced by the surfers of Newquay.

People from all over the earth came to see the famous surfing seal.

Sid was the happiest seal in all the world, living his dreams everyday surfing and making friends!

It's hard not to smile when you see Sid surfing with the humans.
His joy and enthusiasm are infectious, and his talent on a board is truly impressive.

Sid has become an ambassador for the surfing community and a new best friend to all that meet him, proving that anyone - even a surfing seal - can find their place in the world.

The End

Joseph was born and raised in the South West of England by the seaside, where his love of the ocean began. He is a father, husband and avid surfer. This story was inspired by a chance encounter with a seal whilst surfing at Towan Beach in Newquay during a winter storm, this was the first of many!

Jon was born in Hampshire but now lives in Derby with his wife, son and two cats. He has always loved to draw and started doing so digitally during lockdown. A cup of coffee, some lofi music and family close by is what makes it all work.

Seals are beautiful and endearing creatures but remember...

If you see a seal in the wild please never try to approach them, touch them or move them back into the sea. This can be dangerous and extremely stressful for the seal.

If you are worried about a seal, the best way to help is to watch it from a distance then contact your local animal charity or organisation such as the RSPCA, Seal Alliance, etc.

If the seals are looking at you, then you're too close and you'll need to back away quietly.

Keep up to date and look out for more upcoming adventures with Sid the Seal!

www.sidtheseal.co.uk

Info@sidtheseal.co.uk

📷 @sidthesealbooks

f @sidthesealbooks

Follow Jon:

📷 @scribblesaurus23

f @Jonathan Foard

Printed in Great Britain
by Amazon

33005093R00016